SOUND THEF
BEGINNERS

Simple Techniques with Healing Sounds,
Frequencies, and Vibrations for Stress
Relief and Calm

Lily Penrose

Sound Therapy for Beginners: *Simple Techniques with Healing Sounds, Frequencies, and Vibrations for Stress Relief and Calm* By Lily Penrose

First Edition, 2025

TABLE OF CONTENTS

INTRODUCTION TO SOUND THERAPY

Understanding Sound Therapy

Sound therapy is a practice that harnesses the power of sound and vibration to promote healing and relaxation. It is based on the idea that everything in the universe vibrates at a specific frequency, including our bodies and emotions. By using specific sounds, frequencies, and vibrations, individuals can create a harmonious environment that fosters emotional balance and reduces stress. This approach is accessible to everyone and can be easily integrated into daily routines for significant benefits.

One of the most popular methods of sound therapy includes listening to nature soundscapes. These soothing sounds, such as rain, ocean waves, or birdsong, can transport listeners to a tranquil state, making them an excellent tool for relaxation. Nature sounds are known to reduce anxiety and enhance mood, making them a perfect addition to any stress relief routine. With just a few minutes of listening, individuals can feel more grounded and at peace.

Tibetan singing bowls are another powerful tool in sound therapy. These bowls produce a rich, resonant sound that can help to calm the mind and body. When struck or circled with a mallet, they create vibrations that resonate throughout the body, promoting deep relaxation and emotional release. Many people find that incorporating singing bowls into meditation practices enhances their experience, allowing for a deeper connection to self and inner peace.

Binaural beats offer a unique approach to sound therapy, especially for those seeking improved sleep. By playing two slightly different frequencies in each ear, the brain creates a third frequency that can induce various states of relaxation. This technique is especially useful for individuals struggling with insomnia or anxiety, as it encourages the brain to enter a restful state. Listening to binaural beats before bed can significantly enhance sleep quality and overall well-being.

Finally, DIY sound therapy tools can empower individuals to create their own healing spaces at home. Simple techniques such as chanting, vocal toning, or using crystal singing bowls can be easily learned and practiced. By integrating these sound therapy techniques into daily life, individuals can cultivate a personal sanctuary for stress relief and emotional balance, promoting a healthier lifestyle overall.

The Science Behind Sound and Healing

The fascinating relationship between sound and healing is deeply rooted in science, revealing how different frequencies can influence our physical and emotional well-being. Sound waves travel in vibrations, impacting our environment and our bodies in ways that can promote relaxation and reduce stress. When we listen to calming sounds, like nature soundscapes or Tibetan singing bowls, our brain waves can synchronize with these frequencies, leading to a more tranquil state of mind. This connection between sound and healing is not just anecdotal; it is supported by research in fields such as psychology and neuroscience.

One of the key elements in sound therapy is the concept of resonance. Resonance occurs when an object or system vibrates at a specific frequency, amplifying the sound and enhancing its effects. For instance, when we use crystal bowls or other sound therapy instruments, the vibrations resonate within our bodies, potentially aligning our chakras and promoting emotional balance. This principle underscores why certain sounds can evoke profound feelings of peace and relaxation, making them effective tools for stress relief.

Binaural beats are another powerful sound therapy technique that harnesses the science of sound for healing. By playing two slightly different frequencies in each ear, the brain perceives a third frequency, which can help induce states of relaxation, focus, or deep sleep. This method is particularly useful for those struggling with anxiety or insomnia, as it provides a non-invasive way to enhance mental well-being. Integrating binaural beats into daily routines can create a calming atmosphere that promotes emotional stability.

Chanting and vocal toning techniques also play a significant role in sound therapy. The act of vocalizing produces vibrations that can not only resonate within the body but also create a sense of community and connection when practiced in groups. These techniques can be easily incorporated into family activities, making them accessible for both adults and children. The shared experience of sound can foster emotional healing and strengthen relationships, highlighting the importance of sound in our everyday lives.

Finally, the DIY aspect of sound therapy allows individuals to explore and create their own healing tools at home. Whether through making simple instruments or using everyday objects to generate sound, the possibilities are endless. This empowerment encourages personal exploration and the development of a unique sound therapy practice that suits individual needs. By embracing the science behind sound and its healing properties, anyone can cultivate a more harmonious and balanced life.

The Benefits of Sound Therapy for Stress Relief

Sound therapy provides a simple yet powerful approach to relieving stress, making it an invaluable tool for adults seeking balance and tranquility in their lives. By utilizing various sound techniques, individuals can tap into the healing frequencies that resonate with their bodies, promoting relaxation and emotional well-being. Whether it's through soothing nature soundscapes or the enchanting tones of Tibetan singing bowls, these auditory experiences can significantly diminish the impact of daily stressors.

One of the most appealing aspects of sound therapy is its accessibility. Adults can easily incorporate sound healing into their daily routines, whether by listening to binaural beats for enhanced sleep or engaging in guided sound meditation for anxiety relief. The beauty of these practices lies in their simplicity; they require no technical expertise, allowing anyone to experience the calming effects of sound. This makes sound therapy an ideal choice for those who may feel overwhelmed by more complex stress management techniques.

In addition to promoting relaxation, sound therapy also aids in emotional balance. Techniques such as chanting and vocal toning provide an expressive outlet for emotions, helping individuals to release pent-up feelings and restore inner peace. Crystal healing combined with sound frequencies further amplifies this emotional release, as the vibrations from the crystals harmonize with the sounds, creating a profound sense of clarity and calmness.

Moreover, sound therapy can be a family activity, making it inclusive for all ages. By introducing children to sound healing through playful DIY sound therapy tools or family sound baths, parents can instill a sense of mindfulness and relaxation from a young age. This not only strengthens family bonds but also equips future generations with effective tools for managing stress.

Ultimately, the benefits of sound therapy extend beyond mere relaxation. It serves as a holistic approach to achieving emotional balance, stress relief, and overall well-being. By embracing the healing power of sound and vibration, individuals can cultivate a more peaceful existence, enhancing their quality of life in a simple yet profound manner.

HEALING SOUNDS AND FREQUENCIES

The Power of Frequencies

The concept of frequencies is fundamental in understanding how sound affects our well-being. Every sound, whether it is a gentle breeze or a Tibetan singing bowl, vibrates at a specific frequency. These frequencies can influence our emotional state, helping us to relax, relieve stress, and find balance in our lives. By tapping into these natural vibrations, we can enhance our mental and emotional health in simple and accessible ways.

Different frequencies resonate with various aspects of our being. For example, lower frequencies may evoke a sense of calm and grounding, while higher frequencies can uplift our spirits and inspire creativity. Sound therapy utilizes these principles, allowing us to choose sounds that align with our needs at any given moment. This empowers us to take control of our emotional landscape, using sound as a tool for healing and transformation.

Nature soundscapes, such as rain falling or waves crashing, are prime examples of how frequencies from the environment can soothe our minds. By integrating these natural sounds into our daily routines, we can create a peaceful atmosphere that promotes relaxation and mindfulness. Listening to these frequencies can transport us to a place of tranquility, making it easier to cope with the stresses of everyday life.

In addition to nature sounds, techniques like binaural beats and chanting can further enhance our experience with sound therapy. Binaural beats, for instance, work by playing two slightly different frequencies in each ear, encouraging the brain to synchronize with the beats. This can lead to improved sleep and reduced anxiety. Similarly, vocal toning and chanting can create a powerful resonance within our bodies, helping to align our chakras and promote emotional balance.

Ultimately, the power of frequencies lies in their ability to connect us to our inner selves and the world around us. By exploring various sound therapy techniques, we can discover which frequencies resonate with us personally. This journey not only enriches our understanding of sound but also provides valuable tools for achieving relaxation, emotional balance, and overall well-being.

Exploring Healing Sounds

Healing sounds play a vital role in promoting relaxation and emotional balance. Through various techniques, individuals can harness the power of sound to alleviate stress and create a serene environment. Whether it's the gentle hum of nature soundscapes or the soothing tones of Tibetan singing bowls, each sound offers unique benefits that can enhance overall well-being.

One of the simplest ways to integrate healing sounds into daily life is through guided sound meditation. This practice encourages mindfulness and helps individuals connect with their inner selves. By focusing on specific frequencies and vibrations, one can experience profound relaxation, making it an excellent tool for managing anxiety and stress.

Binaural beats are another fascinating technique that utilizes sound frequencies to promote better sleep and relaxation. By playing two slightly different frequencies in each ear, the brain perceives a third tone that can lead to deeper states of calm. This method has gained popularity among those seeking an effective way to improve sleep quality and reduce nighttime anxiety.

Chanting and vocal toning techniques also offer a unique avenue for healing. The vibrational quality of the human voice can resonate with the body's energy centers, or chakras, facilitating a sense of balance and harmony. Engaging in these practices can be both empowering and soothing, allowing individuals to express themselves while experiencing the therapeutic effects of sound.

Finally, creating DIY sound therapy tools at home can make the healing process accessible to everyone. Simple instruments like rattles or drums can be easily crafted, providing a personal touch to the sound therapy experience. By incorporating these tools into family routines, sound therapy can become a shared journey toward relaxation and emotional wellness, fostering connection and harmony within the household.

How to Use Sound for Emotional Balance

Sound has a profound effect on our emotional state, and utilizing it can lead to remarkable benefits for our mental well-being. One of the simplest methods to achieve emotional balance is through listening to nature soundscapes. The soothing sounds of rain, ocean waves, or birds chirping can transport us to a place of tranquility, helping to reduce stress and create a peaceful atmosphere. These natural frequencies resonate with our inner selves, allowing us to reconnect with the world around us and instill a sense of calm.

Another effective approach is using Tibetan singing bowls, which produce rich, harmonious tones that can aid in meditation and relaxation. When struck, these bowls emit vibrations that penetrate deep into our bodies, promoting a sense of peace and emotional release. Incorporating these bowls into a regular meditation practice can enhance your experience, making it easier to let go of anxiety and invite emotional balance into your life.

Binaural beats are another fascinating tool for emotional regulation. By playing two slightly different frequencies in each ear, our brain perceives a third tone, which can help induce various states of consciousness. This technique can be particularly useful for sleep enhancement or deep relaxation, as it encourages the brain to synchronize with the rhythm of the beats, leading to a more balanced emotional state and better stress management.

Chanting and vocal toning techniques provide an additional avenue for emotional healing. By using your voice to produce sound, you can release pent-up emotions and create a sense of harmony within yourself. Whether you choose to chant mantras or simply hum, the vibrations produced can resonate through your body, promoting a feeling of connectedness and emotional stability.

Finally, integrating sound therapy into your daily routine can create lasting changes in your emotional health. Whether it's setting aside time for guided sound meditation or experimenting with DIY sound therapy tools at home, making sound a regular part of your life can help maintain emotional balance. The key is to find what resonates with you personally, allowing sound and vibration to support your journey toward relaxation and emotional well-being.

NATURE SOUNDSCAPES FOR RELAXATION

The Healing Power of Nature Sounds

The healing power of nature sounds has been recognized for centuries, influencing various cultures and healing practices. From the gentle rustling of leaves in the wind to the calming rhythm of ocean waves, these natural soundscapes serve as a backdrop for relaxation and rejuvenation. When we immerse ourselves in these soothing sounds, our bodies respond positively, reducing stress levels and promoting a sense of peace. This connection to nature through sound not only encourages relaxation but also enhances our emotional well-being, making it an invaluable tool for stress relief in our busy lives.

Incorporating nature sounds into your daily routine can be as simple as taking a moment to listen to a recording of a forest or beach. These soundscapes can be played softly in the background while you work, meditate, or unwind after a long day. Many people find that these sounds help them concentrate better, creating a tranquil atmosphere that fosters productivity. Furthermore, the use of nature sounds in combination with other sound therapy techniques, such as Tibetan singing bowls or binaural beats, can amplify the benefits, allowing for deeper relaxation and emotional balance.

Research shows that exposure to natural sounds can lower blood pressure, decrease anxiety, and even improve sleep quality. This is particularly relevant in today's fast-paced world, where stress and anxiety levels are on the rise. Nature sounds serve as a reminder of the calmness and beauty of the natural world, helping to ground us and bring us back to the present moment. Embracing these sounds can lead to a profound transformation in our mental and emotional health, providing a sanctuary of peace amid life's chaos.

For those exploring sound therapy, creating your own nature sound environment can be a rewarding experience. You can use simple DIY sound therapy tools, such as jars filled with pebbles or rice to mimic the sound of rain, or even your voice to chant and tone. Integrating these elements into your home creates a personalized sanctuary where you can retreat whenever you feel overwhelmed. This hands-on approach not only enhances your connection to the sounds but also empowers you to take control of your own healing journey.

Ultimately, the healing power of nature sounds lies in their ability to connect us to our surroundings and our inner selves. By embracing these soothing audio experiences, we can cultivate a sense of emotional balance and well-being. Whether through guided sound meditation, gentle soundscapes, or simply enjoying the sounds of nature, incorporating these practices into our lives can lead to profound changes, allowing us to navigate our daily stresses with greater ease and calm.

Creating Your Own Nature Soundscape

Creating your own nature soundscape can be a profoundly therapeutic experience, allowing you to connect with the calming forces of nature from the comfort of your home. Start by identifying the types of natural sounds that resonate with you, such as the gentle rustling of leaves, the rhythmic crashing of ocean waves, or the soothing chirping of birds. With a little creativity and intention, you can curate a sound environment that promotes relaxation and emotional balance.

To begin crafting your soundscape, explore the various resources available for capturing or generating these sounds. You can use recording devices to capture sounds from your local environment, or turn to online platforms that offer high-quality nature sound recordings. Additionally, consider using sound therapy tools such as Tibetan singing bowls to complement your natural sounds, as their vibrations can enhance the overall experience and deepen relaxation.

Another method to create your own soundscape is through layering different sounds. For instance, you might combine the sound of a flowing stream with the soft calls of distant birds, creating a rich auditory tapestry that transports you to a peaceful natural setting. Experiment with the volume levels and timing of each sound to find a blend that feels harmonious and soothing to you.

Incorporating guided sound meditation can also enhance your nature soundscape. You might find recordings that guide you through a meditative experience while immersing you in the sounds of nature. This practice can help you focus your mind, alleviate anxiety, and promote a deeper sense of calm, making it easier to access a state of relaxation whenever you need it.

Lastly, consider making this process a part of your daily routine. Set aside a few moments each day to immerse yourself in your personalized soundscape, whether through listening or participating in a meditative practice. By integrating these nature sounds into your life, you can create a sanctuary of peace and tranquility, helping you navigate the stresses of daily life with greater ease.

Integrating Nature Sounds into Daily Life

Incorporating nature sounds into daily life can significantly enhance emotional well-being and promote relaxation. The gentle rustling of leaves, the soft chirping of birds, or the calming flow of a nearby stream can create a peaceful atmosphere that helps to reduce stress. By intentionally integrating these natural soundscapes into our routines, we can foster a sense of tranquility that permeates our busy lives. Whether it's during morning meditation or winding down in the evening, the sounds of nature provide a comforting backdrop that encourages mindfulness and presence.

One simple way to incorporate nature sounds is by using sound apps or playlists that feature high-quality recordings of outdoor environments. These resources allow you to create a personalized sound environment that suits your mood and needs. For instance, listening to ocean waves can evoke feelings of peace and relaxation, while birdsong may uplift your spirits and foster a sense of joy. By experimenting with different soundscapes, you can discover which ones resonate most with you and enhance your daily experiences.

Another effective method is to bring nature sounds into your physical space. Consider placing a small water fountain in your home or office, as the sound of flowing water can be incredibly soothing. Alternatively, open a window or spend time outdoors to immerse yourself in the natural sounds around you. Even during busy days, taking a moment to pause and listen to the sounds of nature can significantly shift your mindset and promote a sense of calm.

Mindful breathing exercises combined with nature sounds can further enhance relaxation. As you listen to the gentle rhythm of a forest or a rainstorm, focus on your breath, allowing your inhalations and exhalations to synchronize with the sounds. This practice not only deepens your connection to the natural world but also aids in grounding and centering your thoughts. Incorporating these techniques into your daily routine can provide profound emotional balance and stress relief.

Finally, consider sharing nature sounds with loved ones as a way to bond and create shared moments of peace. Playing calming nature sounds during family gatherings or quiet evenings can help set a serene atmosphere. Engaging in sound therapy together fosters deeper connections and encourages open conversations about emotional well-being. By integrating nature sounds into your daily life, you cultivate a nurturing environment that supports relaxation and emotional harmony.

TIBETAN SINGING BOWLS FOR MEDITATION

History and Significance of Tibetan Singing Bowls

Tibetan singing bowls have a rich history that spans centuries, originating from the Himalayan region of Tibet. These bowls are made from a unique alloy of metals, often including bronze, and are hand-hammered to create their distinctive sound. Traditionally, they were used by monks in spiritual rituals, healing practices, and meditation. The deep, resonant tones produced by striking or rubbing the bowls are believed to connect the user with their inner self and promote a sense of tranquility.

The significance of Tibetan singing bowls extends beyond their auditory beauty; they are integral to various healing practices. These bowls are often utilized in sound therapy sessions to help individuals achieve emotional balance and relaxation. The vibrations emitted by the bowls are thought to resonate with the body's energy centers, or chakras, facilitating healing and restoring harmony. This connection to ancient healing traditions makes singing bowls a vital tool for modern sound therapy.

As more people seek natural ways to relieve stress and promote relaxation, the popularity of Tibetan singing bowls has surged. Adults looking for simple, non-technical approaches to sound therapy find these bowls particularly appealing. Whether used during meditation, yoga, or simply for personal relaxation, the bowls provide an accessible means to experience the calming effects of sound. Their ability to create a peaceful atmosphere makes them a favorite in wellness settings around the world.

In addition to their therapeutic uses, Tibetan singing bowls also serve as a reminder of the beauty of mindfulness. Engaging with these bowls encourages individuals to slow down and be present in the moment. The act of playing a singing bowl can be a meditative practice in itself, allowing users to focus on the sound and vibration while letting go of distractions. This mindful engagement fosters a deeper connection to oneself and the surrounding environment.

In summary, the history and significance of Tibetan singing bowls lie in their unique ability to bridge ancient healing traditions with modern practices for stress relief and emotional balance. Their resonant sounds not only promote relaxation but also encourage mindfulness and self-awareness. By integrating Tibetan singing bowls into daily routines, individuals can enhance their well-being and cultivate a deeper sense of peace in their lives.

How to Use Singing Bowls for Meditation

Singing bowls have been used for centuries as tools for meditation and healing. Their resonant tones and vibrations can help create a peaceful atmosphere, making them an excellent addition to your meditation practice. To begin using singing bowls for meditation, find a quiet space where you can sit comfortably. Ensure you won't be disturbed, and take a moment to settle into your surroundings.

Once you are comfortable, hold the singing bowl in your lap or place it on a soft surface. Use a mallet to gently strike the bowl, producing a clear, ringing sound. As the sound resonates, allow yourself to focus on the vibrations. Close your eyes and take deep breaths, letting the sound wash over you, which can help quiet the mind and promote relaxation.

After striking the bowl, you can also run the mallet around the rim to create a continuous tone. This sustained sound can deepen your meditation experience. Pay attention to how the vibrations feel in your body; some may resonate with your heart or throat, helping to release tension or emotional blockages. Let these sensations guide you deeper into your meditative state.

Incorporating singing bowls into your meditation routine can enhance your emotional balance and relieve stress. Experiment with different bowls, as each has a unique tone and vibration that may resonate with you differently. Additionally, consider pairing the bowls with guided sound meditations or nature soundscapes to enrich your sessions further.

As you practice regularly, you may notice a greater sense of calm and clarity in your daily life. Singing bowls not only serve as an effective meditation tool but also as a way to connect with yourself on a deeper level. Embrace the journey of sound therapy, and let the healing vibrations of singing bowls support your path to relaxation and emotional well-being.

Experiencing the Vibrations of Sound

Sound has an incredible ability to affect our emotions and well-being, acting as a powerful tool for relaxation and stress relief. When we experience the vibrations of sound, whether through music, nature soundscapes, or sound therapy tools like Tibetan singing bowls, we tap into a universal language that resonates with our inner selves. This subchapter explores how these vibrations can enhance our daily lives, promoting emotional balance and relaxation in simple, accessible ways.

One of the most soothing experiences comes from immersing ourselves in nature soundscapes. The gentle rustling of leaves, the melodic chirping of birds, and the calming flow of water create an atmosphere that encourages peace and mindfulness. By incorporating these sounds into our daily routines, we can find moments of tranquility that help ground us amidst the chaos of everyday life. Listening to nature sounds can transport us to serene environments, making it easier to release tension and foster inner calm.

Tibetan singing bowls offer another profound avenue for experiencing sound vibrations. When struck or circled with a mallet, these bowls produce harmonic tones that resonate deeply within the body. This resonance can help release stuck energy, promote relaxation, and even facilitate meditation. By finding a quiet space, closing our eyes, and allowing the sounds to wash over us, we invite a sense of peace and healing into our lives.

Binaural beats are another fascinating aspect of sound therapy that utilize the brain's ability to process different frequencies. By listening to two slightly different frequencies in each ear, the brain creates a third tone, which can induce various states of relaxation, focus, or even sleep enhancement. This technique is easy to integrate into our daily routines, whether during meditation, as a sleep aid, or simply for a moment of stress relief.

Lastly, integrating vocal techniques like chanting and toning into our sound experiences can deepen our connection to the vibrations around us. Our voices can create powerful sound waves that resonate within our bodies, helping to balance our energy and elevate our mood. This practice can be as simple as humming a favorite tune or joining a group chant, allowing us to harness the healing power of sound in community and solitude alike. By exploring these various sound modalities, we can cultivate a richer emotional landscape and find greater balance in our lives.

BINAURAL BEATS FOR SLEEP ENHANCEMENT

Understanding Binaural Beats

Binaural beats are a fascinating auditory phenomenon that can significantly enhance relaxation and mental well-being. When two slightly different frequencies are played in each ear, the brain perceives a third tone, which is the difference between the two. This unique sound experience can help individuals achieve a state of calm and focus, making it a popular choice for those seeking stress relief through sound therapy.

The science behind binaural beats lies in how our brain processes sound. When the brain detects these two frequencies, it naturally synchronizes its brainwave activity to match the perceived beat. This process, known as brainwave entrainment, can lead to various mental states, such as relaxation, meditation, or even deeper sleep. By choosing specific frequency ranges, users can target their desired state of mind, whether it's for anxiety relief or enhanced concentration.

To experience binaural beats, one needs a pair of headphones and a quiet space. Many apps and online platforms offer pre-recorded binaural beats tailored for different purposes, including sleep enhancement and emotional balance. Listening to these tracks for just a few minutes daily can yield significant benefits, providing a simple yet effective way to incorporate sound therapy into one's routine.

For those interested in exploring sound therapy further, binaural beats can be combined with other techniques, such as guided meditations or nature soundscapes. This integration creates a rich auditory experience that not only enhances relaxation but also supports overall emotional health. The versatility of binaural beats makes them an excellent tool for both beginners and experienced practitioners in the field of sound therapy.

Ultimately, understanding binaural beats opens the door to a world of auditory healing. They offer a non-invasive, accessible method to harness the power of sound for personal wellness. As more people seek natural ways to manage stress and cultivate emotional balance, binaural beats stand out as a profound yet simple solution that anyone can embrace.

Using Binaural Beats for Better Sleep

Binaural beats are an innovative sound therapy technique that can significantly enhance sleep quality. By playing two slightly different frequencies in each ear, binaural beats create a third perceived frequency in the brain. This auditory illusion encourages the brain to synchronize its activity to the beat, promoting relaxation and a sense of calm, which is essential for a good night's sleep. Many adults seeking simple methods to manage stress and achieve emotional balance have found success with this approach.

Incorporating binaural beats into your nightly routine can be as easy as listening to a specialized audio track before bed. There are various types of binaural beats designed specifically for sleep enhancement, often featuring soothing soundscapes that mimic nature. These can include gentle rain, flowing water, or soft instrumental music, all harmoniously blended with the binaural beats. This combination not only aids in falling asleep faster but also helps in maintaining uninterrupted sleep throughout the night.

To maximize the benefits of binaural beats, it's important to create an ideal listening environment. This means finding a quiet, comfortable space where you can relax without distractions. You may want to use headphones to ensure that each ear receives the correct frequency, allowing the beats to work effectively. Dim lighting or the use of calming scents like lavender can further enhance the ambiance, making your sleep experience even more restorative.

Many people find that setting a specific time each night for their binaural beats session helps signal to the body that it's time to wind down. This habit can train your brain to associate the sound with relaxation and sleep, making it easier to drift off. Additionally, combining binaural beats with other relaxation techniques, such as deep breathing or gentle stretching, can amplify their effects, promoting an even deeper sense of peace before sleep.

As you explore the world of binaural beats, remember that consistency is key. It may take some time to discover the specific frequencies and soundscapes that resonate best with you. By integrating binaural beats into your nightly routine, you can transform your sleep experience, leading to improved overall well-being and emotional balance. Embrace this simple yet powerful tool and unlock the potential for better rest and rejuvenation with the soothing power of sound.

Creating a Binaural Beats Playlist

Creating a binaural beats playlist can be an enriching experience that enhances your journey into sound therapy. Start by understanding the different frequencies associated with various states of mind. For instance, Delta waves (0.5 - 4 Hz) are linked to deep sleep, while Alpha waves (8 - 12 Hz) promote relaxation and creativity. Identifying your desired outcome will guide you in selecting the right tracks for your playlist.

Once you have a clear idea of the frequencies you want to include, explore platforms that offer high-quality binaural beats tracks. There are numerous online resources, including streaming services and dedicated sound therapy websites, where you can find curated playlists. Pay attention to the length of the tracks as well; longer sessions are often more effective for deep relaxation or meditation.

When you start assembling your playlist, consider incorporating a variety of sounds and styles. Mixing binaural beats with nature soundscapes, like rain or ocean waves, can create a soothing ambiance. Additionally, you might want to add Tibetan singing bowls or gentle instrumental music to enhance the overall experience, providing a richer sound landscape.

Testing your playlist is essential to ensure it meets your needs. Spend some time listening to the tracks in different settings, whether you're meditating, working, or winding down at the end of the day. Adjust the playlist as necessary, swapping out tracks that do not resonate with you or add to your desired state of relaxation or focus.

Finally, consider the setting in which you listen to your binaural beats playlist. A quiet, comfortable space free from distractions will enhance the effectiveness of the sound therapy. Use headphones to experience the full effect of binaural beats, as they rely on sound being delivered separately to each ear. Over time, you'll find a combination of tracks that supports your emotional balance and stress relief, making your sound therapy practice a personal and transformative journey.

CHANTING AND VOCAL TONING TECHNIQUES

The Power of Your Voice

Your voice is one of the most powerful tools you possess. It is not just a means of communication; it is a source of healing and transformation. When you use your voice consciously, you can create vibrations that resonate within your body and in the environment around you. This resonance can help relieve stress, promote relaxation, and restore emotional balance. By tapping into the power of your voice, you can embark on a journey toward enhanced well-being and inner peace.

Chanting is a simple yet profound technique that demonstrates the power of sound. When you chant, you engage with the rhythm and frequency of your own voice, which can induce a meditative state. This practice has been used across cultures for centuries as a method to connect with oneself and the universe. Whether you choose to chant traditional mantras or simply express sounds that feel good to you, the act of vocalization can release tension and promote a sense of calm.

Vocal toning is another technique that harnesses the power of your voice. By producing sustained sounds at different pitches, you can stimulate energy centers in your body, known as chakras. Each sound corresponds to a specific chakra, helping to balance and align your energy. This practice not only aids in emotional healing but also fosters a deep connection with your inner self, allowing you to express your true feelings and desires.

Incorporating your voice into guided sound meditations can also enhance relaxation. These meditations often include spoken guidance, accompanied by soothing sounds or music. As you follow along, your voice can join in to create a harmonious blend of vibrations that envelops you. This collective sound experience can deepen your sense of security and belonging while encouraging emotional release and self-discovery.

To make sound therapy a part of your daily routine, consider setting aside time to explore your voice. Whether through singing, chanting, or simply speaking affirmations, the act of engaging your voice can be a powerful tool for stress relief and emotional balance. Remember, your voice is a gift—embrace it, express it, and allow it to guide you towards a more peaceful and fulfilled life.

Simple Chanting Techniques for Relaxation

Chanting is a powerful and accessible technique for relaxation that can be easily integrated into daily life. By producing sound with intention, we create vibrations that resonate within our bodies, promoting a sense of calm and emotional balance. Simple chanting techniques can be practiced anywhere, making them an ideal tool for adults seeking stress relief.

One effective method is to choose a simple mantra or phrase to repeat. This could be a word that embodies tranquility, such as "peace" or "calm." As you chant this word, focus on your breath and allow the sound to fill your mind. The repetition helps to quiet the thoughts that often contribute to stress, fostering a deeper state of relaxation.

Another technique involves using your voice to create soothing tones. Start by humming a comfortable pitch, allowing the vibrations to resonate in your chest and throat. This not only feels physically comforting but also helps to shift your mental state. Experiment with different pitches and lengths of hums, finding what feels most relaxing for you.

Incorporating nature sounds can enhance your chanting experience. For instance, you might listen to recordings of gentle rain or ocean waves while you chant. The combination of your voice with these natural soundscapes creates a harmonious environment that deepens relaxation and promotes emotional well-being.

Lastly, consider joining a community group or online class focused on chanting. Shared vocalization can amplify the benefits, as sound waves produced collectively create a powerful sense of unity and support. Engaging with others can also inspire you to explore new chanting techniques and deepen your practice.

Exploring Vocal Toning for Healing

Vocal toning is a powerful yet simple technique that utilizes the voice as an instrument for healing and relaxation. By producing specific sounds and vibrations, individuals can tap into their innate ability to release tension and restore emotional balance. This practice can easily be integrated into daily routines, making it accessible for anyone seeking stress relief without the need for complex instruments or technical knowledge.

One of the most beautiful aspects of vocal toning is its grounding nature. As you begin to experiment with different sounds, you may find that your body instinctively resonates with certain frequencies. This resonance can help align your energy centers, or chakras, promoting a sense of harmony within. Whether you choose to hum, chant, or create vocal melodies, the act of using your voice can lead to profound relaxation and emotional clarity.

Incorporating vocal toning into your meditation practice can also enhance your experience. As you sit in stillness, allow your voice to flow freely, producing soothing sounds that echo through your space. This creates a soundscape that not only calms the mind but also encourages deeper states of consciousness. Whether you are in a quiet room or surrounded by nature, vocal toning can amplify your connection to the present moment.

Additionally, vocal toning can be a communal practice, bringing people together through shared sound. Group toning sessions can foster a sense of unity and collective healing, as participants harmonize their voices to create a rich tapestry of vibrations. This shared experience can be incredibly uplifting, promoting emotional release and a sense of belonging.

For those new to vocal toning, starting with simple sounds is key. You can begin by exploring the vowels—A, E, I, O, U— allowing your voice to flow naturally. Over time, you may develop your unique toning style that resonates with your personal healing journey. Remember, there are no right or wrong sounds in this practice; the goal is to express yourself freely and experience the transformative power of your own voice.

CRYSTAL HEALING AND SOUND FREQUENCIES

The Relationship Between Crystals and Sound

Crystals and sound have long been intertwined in various healing traditions, each complementing the other to promote well-being. The natural vibrational frequencies of crystals can enhance the effects of sound therapy, creating a harmonious environment conducive to relaxation and emotional balance. When sound waves interact with crystalline structures, they can amplify intentions and healing energies, making the combination of sound and crystals a powerful tool for those seeking stress relief.

The unique properties of different crystals resonate at specific frequencies, which can be matched with various sound therapies. For instance, clear quartz is known for its ability to amplify sound vibrations, making it an excellent companion for sound healing practices such as Tibetan singing bowls or binaural beats. By placing crystals around you during a sound therapy session, you can create a resonant field that enhances the overall experience, promoting deeper relaxation and a stronger connection to your intentions.

Sound therapy techniques like chanting or vocal toning can also be effectively paired with crystal healing. As you engage in these practices, the vibrations from your voice can interact with the frequencies of the crystals, creating a rich tapestry of sound that resonates within you. This synergy can help to release emotional blockages and foster a sense of calm, making it easier to achieve emotional balance and alleviate anxiety.

Incorporating crystals into your daily sound therapy routine can be a simple yet transformative practice. For example, you might choose a specific crystal that aligns with your current emotional needs and hold it while listening to guided sound meditations or nature soundscapes. This integration encourages a deeper connection to the healing properties of both sound and crystals, allowing you to cultivate a sanctuary of peace and tranquility in your life.

Ultimately, the relationship between crystals and sound is about creating a multidimensional approach to wellness. By understanding how these elements work together, you can tailor your sound therapy practices to suit your individual needs, fostering a deeper sense of relaxation and emotional stability. Embrace the power of sound and crystals to unlock a new level of serenity in your life, and let the vibrations guide you on your healing journey.

Choosing Crystals for Sound Therapy

Choosing the right crystals for sound therapy can significantly enhance your experience and effectiveness in achieving relaxation and emotional balance. Each crystal holds unique vibrational frequencies that can resonate with your personal energy, making it essential to select those that align with your intentions. Start by exploring common crystals like clear quartz, amethyst, and rose quartz, each known for their healing properties and compatibility with sound frequencies.

Clear quartz is often referred to as a master healer and is excellent for amplifying sound vibrations. It can enhance the effects of sound therapy by clearing negative energy and promoting a sense of clarity. Pairing clear quartz with sound tools like Tibetan singing bowls or tuning forks can create a powerful synergy, allowing for deeper meditation and relaxation.

Amethyst, with its calming energy, is perfect for those seeking stress relief. This crystal is known for its ability to soothe the mind and promote emotional stability. When combined with gentle sound frequencies, amethyst can help you release tension and foster a peaceful state of mind, making it an ideal choice for guided sound meditation.

Rose quartz, the stone of love, can aid in emotional healing and self-compassion. Its gentle vibrations can be particularly effective when used alongside soft, melodic sounds. Incorporating rose quartz into your sound therapy practice can help you create a nurturing environment, encouraging a connection to your heart space and promoting emotional balance.

As you experiment with different crystals and sound tools, trust your intuition to guide you in making the right choices. Remember that the goal of sound therapy is to create a harmonious environment that supports your journey to relaxation and emotional well-being. By thoughtfully selecting crystals that resonate with your energy, you can deepen your sound therapy practice and enhance the benefits it brings to your life.

Combining Crystals with Sound Techniques

Combining crystals with sound techniques offers a unique approach to enhancing relaxation and emotional balance. The vibrational frequencies of crystals can harmonize beautifully with sound therapies, creating a multi-dimensional healing experience. By understanding how to integrate these elements, individuals can create a soothing atmosphere that promotes well-being and tranquility in their lives.

To begin, it's essential to select crystals that resonate with your intentions. For instance, amethyst is known for its calming properties, while clear quartz amplifies energy. When paired with sound techniques such as Tibetan singing bowls or binaural beats, the synergy can deepen the effects of both the crystal and the sound, making the experience more profound. Simply placing a crystal near a singing bowl while playing it can enhance the vibrational impact, enveloping you in a comforting embrace.

Chanting and vocal toning techniques can also be incredibly effective when combined with crystals. As you vocalize or chant specific sounds, holding a crystal in your hand can help channel your energy and focus your intentions. The resonance created by your voice, along with the crystal's vibrations, can facilitate emotional release and stress relief, allowing for a more immersive meditation experience.

Guided sound meditations incorporating crystals can also be a powerful tool for anxiety relief. As you listen to soothing sounds like nature soundscapes or gentle chimes, visualizing the energy of your chosen crystal can help ground you and enhance your sense of calm. This practice not only aligns your energy with the sounds but also reinforces the healing properties of the crystals, fostering a deeper connection to your inner peace.

Finally, integrating these techniques into your daily routine can significantly impact your overall well-being. Create a dedicated space at home where you can combine sound therapy and crystal healing. Regularly using these methods can help establish a sense of balance and serenity in your life, making it easier to navigate daily stresses and enhancing your emotional resilience.

GUIDED SOUND MEDITATION FOR ANXIETY RELIEF

What is Guided Sound Meditation?

Guided Sound Meditation is a practice that merges the soothing qualities of sound with focused meditation techniques. It invites participants to immerse themselves in a soundscape designed to promote relaxation and emotional balance. By using various sound sources like Tibetan singing bowls, nature soundscapes, and binaural beats, individuals can find a deeper connection to their inner selves and experience profound stress relief. This method is particularly beneficial for those who might find traditional meditation challenging, as the guiding sounds help to anchor the mind and facilitate a tranquil state.

During a guided sound meditation session, participants typically listen to a series of carefully selected sounds that resonate with their emotional and physical needs. The experience often begins with gentle sounds that gradually evolve, allowing the listener to tune into their body and feelings. The vibrations from the sound can help release tension and promote a sense of calm, making it easier to let go of daily stressors. This approach not only enhances relaxation but also aids in achieving emotional balance, which is essential for overall well-being.

The beauty of guided sound meditation lies in its accessibility. Adults seeking simple, non-technical ways to incorporate sound therapy into their lives can easily adopt this practice. Whether done at home or in a group setting, guided sound meditation can be tailored to fit personal preferences and needs. It can also be a wonderful family activity, introducing children to the calming effects of sound and vibration, thereby fostering a supportive environment for emotional growth.

In addition to its immediate benefits, guided sound meditation can also serve as a tool for deeper self-exploration. By engaging with the sounds and allowing them to wash over the mind and body, individuals often discover insights about their emotions and mental states. This reflective aspect can lead to greater emotional awareness and healing, making it a valuable part of a holistic approach to mental health.

For those interested in trying guided sound meditation, there are numerous resources available, including online sessions, recordings, and DIY sound therapy tools. These resources empower individuals to create their own soundscapes at home, helping them integrate sound therapy into their daily routines. As more people recognize the benefits of sound for stress relief and emotional balance, guided sound meditation is becoming an increasingly popular practice for enhancing overall well-being.

Creating Your Own Guided Sound Meditation

Creating your own guided sound meditation can be a transformative experience that enhances your journey into relaxation and emotional balance. Begin by choosing a quiet space where you feel comfortable and safe. This environment will be the backdrop for your meditation, allowing you to focus on the soothing sounds and vibrations that will guide you. Consider the use of nature soundscapes, Tibetan singing bowls, or even your own voice as essential elements that will enrich your meditation.

Next, set a clear intention for your meditation. What do you hope to achieve? Whether it's relief from anxiety, a deeper sense of calm, or a connection to your inner self, having a purpose helps direct your focus. You might want to incorporate specific sound frequencies known for their healing properties, such as those that resonate with chakra balancing. By aligning your intention with the sounds you choose, you create a powerful synergy that enhances the meditation experience.

As you begin your meditation, take a moment to ground yourself. Close your eyes, take a few deep breaths, and let go of any tension in your body. Start by introducing your chosen sounds gradually, allowing them to wash over you. You can layer different sounds, such as gentle chimes, ambient nature sounds, or binaural beats, to create a rich auditory tapestry. This layering can evoke different emotional responses and deepen your sense of relaxation.

Vocal toning or soft chanting can also be a wonderful addition to your guided sound meditation. Using your voice to create sound not only helps in expressing emotions but also generates vibrations that resonate with your body. Experiment with different tones and pitches, and notice how they affect your emotional state. Allow yourself to be free in this practice; there are no wrong notes in your personal meditation.

Finally, conclude your meditation by taking a moment to reflect on your experience. Slowly bring your awareness back to the present moment, feeling gratitude for the journey you just undertook. You may want to journal your thoughts or simply sit in silence for a few more moments. Remember, creating your own guided sound meditation is a personal practice, and with each session, you will deepen your connection to the sounds that promote healing and relaxation in your life.

Tips for a Successful Meditation Session

Creating a successful meditation session requires a serene environment that encourages relaxation and focus. Begin by finding a quiet space where you won't be disturbed. This could be a dedicated room or a cozy corner of your home. Consider the lighting; soft, natural light or subdued lamps can help set a calming mood. You might also want to incorporate elements like cushions or blankets to ensure comfort during your practice. The goal is to craft a setting that feels inviting and tranquil, allowing your mind to settle.

Incorporating sound into your meditation can significantly enhance your experience. Whether you choose Tibetan singing bowls, nature soundscapes, or binaural beats, the right sounds can help you enter a deeper state of relaxation. Experiment with different types of sounds to discover what resonates best with you. For some, the gentle hum of nature sounds might evoke peace, while others may find that the harmonic tones of singing bowls elevate their meditation practice. Allow your chosen sounds to guide you into a space of calm.

Establishing a routine can be beneficial for your meditation practice. Setting aside a specific time each day can help instill the habit and signal to your mind that it's time to unwind. Whether it's early in the morning or just before bed, consistency is key. As you develop this routine, your mind will begin to associate this time with relaxation and stress relief. Over time, you might find that your sessions become increasingly fulfilling and transformative.

During your meditation, it's natural for thoughts to arise. Instead of resisting them, acknowledge them and gently guide your focus back to your breath or the sounds surrounding you. This practice of mindfulness helps to cultivate emotional balance and can lead to deeper insights. Remember, the goal is not to silence your mind completely but to create a space where thoughts can flow without causing distress. Embrace each moment as part of your journey towards inner peace.

Finally, be patient with yourself as you explore sound therapy and meditation. Progress may be gradual, and it's essential to honor your unique experience. Celebrate the small victories, whether it's a feeling of calmness or a moment of clarity. By allowing yourself the grace to grow at your own pace, you will find that your meditation practice becomes a cherished part of your daily routine, bringing you closer to emotional well-being and serenity.

DIY Sound Therapy Tools for Home Use

Simple Instruments You Can Create

Creating simple instruments at home can be a delightful and therapeutic experience. You don't need a music degree or extensive training to explore sound therapy; with just a few materials, you can craft instruments that resonate with your inner self and promote relaxation. For instance, a simple water xylophone made from glasses filled with varying levels of water can produce soothing tones, allowing you to play melodies that calm the mind.

Another easy instrument to make is a rain stick, which can be created from a cardboard tube filled with rice or small beans. As you tilt the stick, the sound of the grains cascading down mimics the gentle patter of rain, creating a serene atmosphere. This instrument not only serves as a sound source but also as a tool for mindfulness, helping you focus on the present moment while enjoying the auditory experience.

Tibetan singing bowls, though traditionally crafted, can also be made at home using metal mixing bowls. By gently striking or rubbing the rim with a mallet, you can create rich, harmonic tones that promote relaxation and meditation. The vibrations produced can help in balancing your chakras and enhancing your emotional well-being, making this a wonderful addition to your sound therapy toolkit.

Chanting and vocal toning are among the simplest forms of sound therapy that require no materials at all. Using your voice, you can create vibrations that resonate within your body, helping to release stress and promote emotional balance. Experimenting with different pitches and tones can lead to a deeply personal and transformative experience, connecting you to your inner self through the power of sound.

Lastly, consider creating a DIY sound bath using everyday items like pots, pans, and even your own voice. By layering different sounds, you can create a rich soundscape that envelops you in a soothing environment. Whether you are using instruments or your voice, these simple creations can become powerful tools for relaxation, stress relief, and emotional healing, easily integrated into your daily routine.

Everyday Items for Sound Therapy

Sound therapy can be easily integrated into daily life using items that are commonly found around the house. Everyday objects can serve as powerful tools for creating sound and vibration that promote relaxation and emotional balance. By tapping into these accessible resources, individuals can harness the therapeutic benefits of sound without the need for specialized equipment or training.

Consider the simple act of using a pot or pan to create rhythmic beats. By striking the surface with a wooden spoon, you can produce a resonant sound that can be calming and grounding. This rhythmic drumming can help release pent-up stress and anxiety, allowing the mind to focus on the present moment. Pairing this activity with deep breathing can enhance its effectiveness, turning an ordinary kitchen item into an effective sound therapy tool.

Another everyday item that can be utilized is a glass or ceramic bowl filled with water. By gently tapping the side of the bowl with a spoon, you can create soothing vibrations that ripple through the water, creating a visual and auditory experience. This can be particularly beneficial for mindfulness practices, as the sound encourages individuals to slow down and connect with their senses. The resonance of the bowl can also promote a sense of calm and clarity.

Chanting is another simple yet profound method to incorporate sound therapy into your routine. Using your own voice, you can explore different tones and frequencies that resonate with your body. This practice not only helps in releasing emotional tension but also fosters a deeper connection with oneself. Even humming softly while engaging in daily tasks can uplift your mood and create a peaceful atmosphere.

Lastly, nature sounds can be an excellent addition to any sound therapy practice. Whether it's the sound of rain tapping on a window or birds chirping outside, these natural soundscapes can enhance relaxation and provide a soothing backdrop for meditation or quiet reflection. By intentionally incorporating these everyday sounds, individuals can create a calming environment that supports their journey toward stress relief and emotional balance.

Setting Up Your Sound Therapy Space

Creating a sound therapy space in your home is a beautiful way to embrace relaxation and emotional balance. The environment you choose should evoke a sense of calm and safety, allowing you to fully immerse yourself in the healing benefits of sound. Start by selecting a quiet area free from distractions, where you can comfortably sit or lie down for your sessions. Consider the size of the space; even a small corner can be transformed into a sanctuary with the right elements in place.

Lighting plays a crucial role in setting the mood for your sound therapy practice. Soft, warm light can create a soothing atmosphere, while natural light can invigorate your spirit. Use candles, lamps, or fairy lights to enhance the ambiance. If you prefer complete darkness for deeper relaxation, blackout curtains can help block out external light. The key is to find a balance that feels inviting and peaceful to you.

Sound elements are central to your therapy space. Whether you choose Tibetan singing bowls, crystal bowls, or recorded nature soundscapes, ensure these tools are easily accessible. Arrange them in a way that feels intuitive, allowing you to flow seamlessly from one technique to another. You might also consider incorporating DIY sound therapy tools like shakers or rainsticks, which can add an interactive element to your practice.

Incorporating nature into your sound therapy space can further enhance the experience. Plants not only purify the air but also bring a sense of tranquility and connection to the earth. Choose low-maintenance varieties that thrive in indoor environments. Additionally, consider adding elements like crystals that resonate with sound frequencies to further balance the energy in your space.

Finally, make your sound therapy area personal. Include items that inspire you, such as meaningful photographs, artwork, or even a journal for reflection. This space is yours to nurture your well-being, so allow it to reflect your personality and preferences. By creating a dedicated sound therapy space, you invite healing, relaxation, and emotional balance into your daily routine, making it easier to integrate these practices into your life.

SOUND THERAPY FOR CHILDREN AND FAMILIES

The Importance of Sound Therapy for Kids

Sound therapy offers valuable benefits for children, particularly in today's fast-paced world. It serves as a gentle approach to enhance emotional well-being and foster relaxation. By incorporating sound therapy into their daily routines, kids can develop better coping mechanisms for stress and anxiety, making it an essential tool for parents seeking to nurture their children's mental health.

One effective method involves utilizing soothing soundscapes, such as nature sounds, which can create a peaceful environment for children. These auditory experiences help reduce overstimulation and promote a sense of calm, allowing kids to unwind and recharge. Simple techniques, such as playing calming music or sounds of nature, can easily be integrated into daily activities, making relaxation a natural part of their lives.

Tibetan singing bowls are another fantastic resource for sound therapy with children. The resonant tones produced by these bowls can be both captivating and soothing, drawing children into a state of mindfulness. Engaging them in this practice not only enhances their focus but also introduces them to the concept of meditation, which can be beneficial for emotional regulation.

Additionally, incorporating vocal techniques such as chanting or toning can empower children to express their feelings more freely. These practices encourage self-expression and creativity while simultaneously providing a therapeutic outlet for any pent-up emotions. Children often find joy in making sounds, and this can lead to increased emotional awareness and resilience.

Ultimately, sound therapy for kids is about creating a nurturing atmosphere where they feel safe to explore their emotions. By integrating sound into their lives, parents can help develop their children's emotional intelligence, enabling them to navigate life's challenges with greater ease. Embracing sound therapy not only benefits children but also fosters deeper connections within families, promoting overall well-being and harmony.

Fun Sound Activities for Families

Sound activities can provide a delightful way for families to bond while exploring the therapeutic benefits of sound and vibration. One simple yet effective activity is creating a nature soundscapes session. Families can gather outdoors or play recorded nature sounds, such as rain or ocean waves, while practicing deep breathing together. This not only helps to calm the mind but also encourages children to connect with the natural world around them, making it a fun and educational experience.

Another enjoyable sound activity is creating DIY musical instruments. Families can craft simple instruments using household items, such as shakers made from rice-filled containers or drums from pots and pans. Once the instruments are ready, everyone can join in a family jam session, allowing each member to express themselves through sound. This fosters creativity and provides a sense of accomplishment as families create their own unique music together.

Chanting and vocal toning are also wonderful activities that can bring families together. By taking turns leading a chant or tone, each member can experience the vibrational benefits of sound while having fun. This practice not only promotes relaxation but also helps strengthen familial bonds as everyone participates in creating a harmonious atmosphere through their voices.

Incorporating guided sound meditation into family routines is another effective way to utilize sound for relaxation. Families can set aside time each week to listen to guided meditations that incorporate soothing sounds. This shared experience can help reduce stress and anxiety while promoting a sense of unity. It's a great opportunity for families to unwind together and learn the importance of mindfulness in their daily lives.

Lastly, families can explore the world of crystal healing and sound frequencies by creating a crystal sound circle. By placing crystals around a central point and playing Tibetan singing bowls or other harmonic sounds, families can experience the powerful vibrations that promote emotional balance. This unique activity not only introduces children to the concept of energy healing but also encourages them to appreciate the calming effects of sound and vibration in their lives.

Creating a Family Sound Ritual

Creating a family sound ritual can be a transformative experience that nurtures connection and fosters emotional balance. Start by selecting a time when all family members can gather in a comfortable space. This could be a cozy living room or a peaceful outdoor area, where the atmosphere is calm and inviting. The goal is to create a safe haven where everyone feels relaxed and open to the healing power of sound.

Begin your sound ritual by incorporating natural soundscapes. You might play recordings of ocean waves, rustling leaves, or gentle rain to set a serene backdrop. These sounds can help everyone transition from the busyness of daily life into a more meditative state. Encourage family members to close their eyes, breathe deeply, and simply absorb the soothing vibrations around them.

Next, introduce simple sound-making tools that everyone can use. Tibetan singing bowls, for instance, are easy to play and produce beautiful resonant tones. You can take turns playing the bowls, allowing each family member to express themselves through sound. This not only promotes creativity but also helps individuals feel heard and valued within the family unit.

Chanting and vocal toning can be powerful additions to your ritual as well. Encourage family members to join in harmonizing simple chants or create their own vocal sounds. This communal expression enhances emotional release and strengthens bonds, creating a shared experience that resonates on a deeper level. Remember, there is no right or wrong way to sound; the focus is on connection and healing.

Finally, conclude your family sound ritual with a moment of silence to reflect on the experience. Invite everyone to share their feelings or insights, fostering open communication and understanding. By integrating these sound practices into your family routine, you cultivate a space for relaxation, stress relief, and emotional balance, enriching your family's collective well-being.

INTEGRATING SOUND THERAPY INTO DAILY ROUTINES

Finding Time for Sound Therapy

Finding time for sound therapy in our busy lives can seem like a daunting task, yet it is essential for maintaining emotional balance and reducing stress. The good news is that sound therapy can be seamlessly integrated into our daily routines without requiring significant adjustments. By designating even a few minutes each day, you can create a powerful practice that enhances your well-being.

Begin by identifying pockets of time throughout your day where sound therapy can fit naturally. Morning rituals, lunchtime breaks, or winding down before bed are ideal moments to incorporate sound. Simple techniques like listening to nature soundscapes or using Tibetan singing bowls can be done while you go about your day, transforming mundane moments into restorative experiences.

For those who find it challenging to carve out dedicated time, consider multitasking with sound therapy. Engage in guided sound meditation while commuting, or play binaural beats in the background as you work. This way, you can enjoy the benefits of sound therapy without needing to set aside extra time; it enhances your current activities instead.

Another effective strategy is to involve family and friends in your sound therapy practice. Group sessions can be a delightful way to bond while benefiting from the calming effects of sound. Whether it's chanting together or creating a DIY sound therapy tool, sharing the experience can deepen your connection and make it more enjoyable.

Ultimately, finding time for sound therapy is about prioritizing your well-being and making small adjustments to your routine. By embracing sound and vibration as tools for relaxation and stress relief, you can cultivate a more harmonious life. Remember, the key is consistency; even a few moments of sound therapy each day can lead to significant improvements in your emotional health.

Sound Therapy in Your Morning Routine

Incorporating sound therapy into your morning routine can be a transformative way to start your day with intention and calm. The gentle vibrations of sound can help to clear your mind, reduce stress, and set a positive tone for the hours ahead. Whether it's the soothing sounds of nature or the resonant tones of Tibetan singing bowls, integrating these elements into your morning can create a sanctuary of peace in your home.

Begin your day by creating a soundscape that resonates with your personal preferences. You might choose to play nature sounds, such as birds chirping or waves crashing, which can evoke feelings of tranquility and connection with the earth. Alternatively, consider using binaural beats to enhance focus and relaxation. These frequencies can help synchronize brainwaves, promoting a state of calm alertness that is perfect for a productive morning.

Next, you might want to incorporate some simple vocal techniques into your routine. Chanting or vocal toning can be an incredibly effective way to release tension and elevate your mood.

Allow your voice to resonate, and feel the vibrations travel through your body as you connect with your inner self. This practice not only calms the mind but also energizes the spirit, making it a fulfilling addition to your morning.

If you have access to crystal singing bowls, consider integrating them into your morning meditation. The harmonic frequencies emitted can aid in chakra balancing, aligning your energy centers for a more harmonious day. Spend a few moments simply sitting with the sound, letting it wash over you and bring clarity to your thoughts and intentions.

Lastly, remember that consistency is key in establishing a sound therapy practice. Make it a ritual to set aside time each morning for these techniques. As you cultivate this habit, you will likely notice a shift in your overall well-being. By starting your day with sound, you create a powerful foundation for stress relief, emotional balance, and a sense of calm that lasts throughout the day.

Evening Sound Practices for Relaxation

Evening sound practices can transform your nightly routine into a tranquil ritual that promotes relaxation and stress relief. As the day winds down, incorporating soothing sounds can create a serene environment that encourages unwinding. Whether it's gentle nature soundscapes or the calming vibrations of Tibetan singing bowls, these practices help signal to your body that it's time to transition into a state of rest and recovery.

One effective technique involves using nature soundscapes, such as the gentle rustling of leaves or the soft murmur of a stream. These sounds evoke a sense of peace and connection to the earth, making it easier to let go of daily tensions. You can play these sounds softly in the background as you settle into your evening routine, allowing their rhythmic patterns to lull your mind into a peaceful state.

In addition to nature sounds, the use of Tibetan singing bowls can significantly enhance your evening relaxation practices. The rich, resonant tones produced by these bowls create a calming atmosphere that invites introspection and mindfulness. By striking a bowl and allowing its vibrations to wash over you, you can release accumulated stress and cultivate a deeper sense of inner peace before sleep.

Another wonderful method to try is the incorporation of binaural beats into your evening sound practices. These auditory illusions can facilitate relaxation and enhance sleep quality by balancing brainwave frequencies. Listening to binaural beats through headphones while lying comfortably in bed can help usher your mind into a tranquil state, preparing your body for a restful night.

Finally, consider utilizing guided sound meditation as part of your evening routine. This practice combines soothing sounds with gentle guidance, allowing you to focus on your breath and release the day's worries. By dedicating a few minutes each evening to this practice, you can cultivate emotional balance and ensure a peaceful night's sleep, paving the way for a refreshed start to the next day.

SOUND FREQUENCIES FOR CHAKRA BALANCING

Understanding Chakras and Their Frequencies

Chakras are energy centers within our bodies that correspond to different aspects of our physical and emotional well-being. Understanding these seven main chakras can enhance our experience of sound therapy, as each chakra resonates with specific frequencies. For instance, the root chakra, located at the base of the spine, is linked to feelings of safety and security, and its frequency is often associated with lower, grounding sounds that can help stabilize emotions and reduce anxiety.

As we move up the chakra system, each energy center connects with a particular frequency that can be influenced by various sound therapies. The sacral chakra, associated with creativity and pleasure, resonates with frequencies that evoke fluid, melodic sounds, which can be particularly effective in fostering emotional release and joy. Similarly, the heart chakra, the center of love and compassion, aligns with higher frequencies that promote healing and emotional balance through soothing vibrations.

Using sound to balance chakras involves identifying the specific frequency that corresponds to each energy center. For example, Tibetan singing bowls can be utilized to resonate with the throat chakra, promoting clear communication and self-expression. Binaural beats, on the other hand, are a modern approach to sound therapy that can assist in harmonizing all chakras by creating an immersive auditory experience that encourages deep relaxation and mindfulness.

Integrating sound therapy into daily routines can also help maintain chakra balance. Simple practices like chanting, vocal toning, or listening to nature soundscapes can create a harmonious environment conducive to emotional healing. DIY sound therapy tools, such as homemade rattles or tuned water bottles, can be fun and effective ways to engage with sound, allowing individuals to explore which frequencies resonate best with their personal energy.

Ultimately, understanding chakras and their frequencies empowers adults to harness the transformative power of sound therapy in their lives. By aligning themselves with these energetic centers, individuals can cultivate a deeper sense of relaxation, stress relief, and emotional well-being. Whether through guided sound meditations or family activities that incorporate sound, the journey toward chakra balance becomes a joyful and enriching part of everyday life.

Techniques for Balancing Your Chakras

Balancing your chakras is an essential aspect of achieving overall well-being and harmony in your life. One effective technique is using sound vibrations, which can resonate with specific chakras to help restore their natural balance. Tibetan singing bowls, for example, produce rich, resonant tones that align beautifully with different energy centers in the body. By simply sitting with the bowl and allowing its sound to wash over you, you can begin to feel the energetic shifts that promote relaxation and emotional clarity.

Another powerful method for chakra balancing involves the use of binaural beats. These sound frequencies create a unique auditory experience that helps to guide your brainwaves into a state conducive to healing and relaxation. By listening to tracks specifically designed for chakra work, you can harmonize your energy centers while effortlessly drifting into a meditative state. This technique is especially useful for individuals seeking a gentle approach to stress relief and emotional balance.

Chanting and vocal toning are also excellent tools for balancing chakras. Each chakra corresponds to a specific sound frequency, and by vocalizing these sounds, you can directly influence your energy flow. Practicing simple chants, whether alone or in a group, can enhance the vibrational experience and foster a sense of community and support. This practice not only aids in chakra alignment but also contributes to overall emotional well-being.

Incorporating nature soundscapes into your chakra balancing routine can deepen your connection to the earth and enhance your meditative experience. Sounds such as flowing water, rustling leaves, or birdsong can serve as a backdrop for your sound therapy sessions, creating a peaceful environment that facilitates relaxation. By blending natural sounds with targeted frequencies, you can cultivate a serene atmosphere that nurtures your mental and emotional health.

Lastly, DIY sound therapy tools, such as tuning forks or crystal singing bowls, allow you to engage actively in your chakra balancing journey. These tools empower you to explore sound healing in a personal and meaningful way, making it accessible for everyday use. As you experiment with different sound frequencies and tools, you will discover what resonates best with your unique energy, leading to a more balanced and harmonious life.

Using Sound to Enhance Chakra Healing

Sound has a profound ability to enhance chakra healing, providing an accessible method for individuals seeking balance and tranquility. Each chakra resonates with specific frequencies that can be activated through sound, enabling a deeper connection to one's inner self. By harnessing the power of sound therapy, adults can explore simple techniques to alleviate stress and promote emotional well-being, ultimately aligning their energies with the natural world around them.

Tibetan singing bowls are one of the most effective tools for chakra healing, producing rich, harmonic tones that resonate with specific energy centers in the body. When played, these bowls create vibrations that can help release blockages and restore balance within the chakras. Incorporating these bowls into a daily practice can transform meditation sessions, making them more profound and impactful as participants feel the vibrations harmonizing their energy fields.

Binaural beats also offer a unique approach to chakra balancing. By listening to two slightly different frequencies in each ear, the brain perceives a third tone, which can help induce states of relaxation or heightened awareness. This method can be particularly beneficial for those struggling with anxiety, as it promotes a calm mind and a focused spirit, allowing for deeper introspection and emotional healing.

Chanting and vocal toning techniques further enhance sound therapy practices, allowing individuals to use their own voice as a powerful healing instrument. Sounds can be channeled to resonate with specific chakras, utilizing the body's natural vibrations to facilitate healing and balance. Engaging in vocal exercises, either alone or in a group, creates a sense of community and shared energy, amplifying the healing effects of sound.

Integrating these sound practices into daily routines can significantly enhance one's overall well-being. Whether through guided sound meditations, nature soundscapes, or DIY sound therapy tools, individuals can find solace and balance amidst the chaos of everyday life. By embracing sound as a healing modality, adults can cultivate a deeper connection to themselves and the world around them, leading to a more harmonious existence.

CONCLUSION AND NEXT STEPS

Embracing Sound Therapy in Your Life

Incorporating sound therapy into your daily life can be a transformative experience. By embracing various sound techniques, you can create a personal sanctuary that promotes relaxation and emotional balance. Whether it's the gentle hum of Tibetan singing bowls or the soothing cadence of nature soundscapes, these auditory experiences can help you unwind and find peace amid the chaos of everyday life.

Exploring different sound modalities is essential in discovering what resonates with you. Binaural beats, for instance, can enhance your sleep quality, guiding you into a restful state with their rhythmic tones. Similarly, vocal toning and chanting can release tension and foster a deep connection to your inner self, allowing you to express emotions that may have been suppressed.

One of the simplest ways to integrate sound therapy into your routine is by using DIY sound tools. Creating your own instruments, such as shakers or wind chimes, allows you to engage with sound on a personal level. These homemade tools can be used during moments of stress or as part of a calming evening ritual, bringing a sense of joy and creativity into your practice.

Involving your family and children in sound therapy can be a delightful way to bond and promote well-being. Guided sound meditations can be tailored for all ages, making it easier to introduce young ones to the benefits of sound. By practicing together, you create a shared space for emotional exploration and healing, contributing to a more harmonious home environment.

Ultimately, the journey of embracing sound therapy is about finding balance and calm in your life. As you explore various frequencies and vibrations, remember that each sound has the potential to heal and uplift. By integrating these practices into your daily routines, you'll cultivate a deeper understanding of yourself and the world around you, enhancing not just your own life but also the lives of those you love.

Continuing Your Sound Therapy Journey

Continuing your sound therapy journey is not just about practicing techniques; it's about embracing a lifestyle that nurtures your mental and emotional well-being. As you explore sound therapy further, consider integrating simple practices into your daily routine. Whether it's listening to nature soundscapes while you work or incorporating Tibetan singing bowls into your meditation sessions, these elements can enhance your relaxation and help you maintain emotional balance.

One of the most accessible ways to continue your journey is through the use of binaural beats, which can aid in enhancing sleep and reducing stress. By simply using headphones, you can experience these soothing frequencies that promote a calm state of mind. Experimenting with different sound frequencies can also bring about positive changes in your mental landscape, encouraging deeper relaxation and focus.

Chanting and vocal toning techniques are powerful tools for emotional release and healing. As you explore these methods, you'll find that they not only help to clear mental clutter but also resonate with your body's energy centers. Integrating these practices into your sound therapy routine can lead to profound experiences of emotional balance and tranquility.

Creating your own DIY sound therapy tools for home use can be an exciting and fulfilling endeavor. Whether you choose to make shakers filled with natural materials or experiment with creating your own guided sound meditations, the process can deepen your connection to sound. This hands-on approach allows you to personalize your sound therapy experience, making it more meaningful and effective.

Lastly, remember that sound therapy can be a wonderful practice to share with children and families. Engaging in sound activities together can foster a serene environment, promoting relaxation and emotional well-being for everyone involved. By maintaining a consistent practice and being open to new experiences, you can create a sound therapy journey that nurtures your spirit and enhances your overall quality of life.

Resources for Further Exploration

Exploring sound therapy can be a transformative journey, and there are numerous resources available to deepen your understanding and practice. Books such as "The Healing Power of Sound" by Mitchell L. Gaynor provide insights into the effects of sound on the body and mind. You can also find online courses that teach various sound healing techniques, from using Tibetan singing bowls to integrating binaural beats into your daily routine. These resources offer a structured approach, making it easier for beginners to get started.

Nature soundscapes are an excellent way to incorporate sound therapy into your life. You can find countless apps and websites dedicated to nature sounds, which can enhance relaxation and reduce stress. Whether it's the sound of rain, ocean waves, or a gentle forest breeze, these recordings can create a serene environment that promotes emotional balance. Listening to these calming sounds can be a simple yet effective tool for mindfulness and grounding.

For those interested in hands-on techniques, workshops and local classes can provide valuable experiences. Many communities offer sessions on sound meditation, chanting, and vocal toning. Participating in these group activities not only enhances your learning but also connects you with like-minded individuals. Engaging directly with sound therapy practices can deepen your understanding and allow you to experience the benefits firsthand.

You might also consider exploring DIY sound therapy tools for home use. Resources such as online tutorials can guide you in creating your own instruments or sound tools, like tuning forks or simple percussion instruments. This hands-on approach can be both fun and therapeutic, allowing you to personalize your sound therapy experience. Integrating sound frequencies into your daily routines becomes easier when you have the tools and knowledge to do so.

Lastly, consider online forums and social media groups where you can discuss your experiences and share insights with others interested in sound therapy. These communities can provide support, encouragement, and additional resources. By engaging with others, you can expand your knowledge and discover new techniques that resonate with you. Remember, the journey into sound therapy is personal and can be enriched by the experiences and wisdom of others.

Thank you for spending this time with me in Sound Therapy for Beginners. I hope these simple practices with healing sounds, vibrations, and frequencies bring more calm, clarity, and balance into your daily life. If you found this book helpful, I would be truly grateful if you shared your thoughts in a review on Amazon. Your feedback not only supports my work, but it also helps other readers discover sound therapy and begin their own journey toward greater peace and wellbeing.

Printed in Dunstable, United Kingdom